PASSIVE INCOME SECRETS

2021

An Easy And Understandable Guide To Top Secret Passive Income Ideas To Make Money Online From Home With Amazon Fba, Drop-Shipping, Affiliate Marketing And Much More

BENJAMIN BLUE

By reading this document, the reader agrees that under no circumstances is the author responsible for any losses, direct or indirect, which are incurred as a result of the use of information contained within this document, including, but not limited to, errors, omissions, or inaccuracies.

Table of Contents

INTRODUCTION

The amount of income you can make is entirely up to you. If you're just looking to earn a few hundred dollars a month you can do it, and if you want to build an online sales empire and become a millionaire in a year, you can do that too. And one of the things that make affiliate marketing fun – is you can do this for any niche you're interested in! So, you can devote your energy toward building a business around your passions, whether its health, dog training, or beauty products!

But let's be clear about what affiliate marketing is not. First off, it's not an MLM scheme. When you do proper affiliate marketing, you are not trying to recruit new members to any kind of system that makes its money through recruitment of salespeople that spend all

their time recruiting other salespeople (or any time, for that matter). If you find some kind of program like that – run!

Affiliate marketing is about selling genuine products. They can be physical products, they can be websites, it could be something like driving traffic to Amazon, or it could be selling a digital product (a video course, on some niche topic, software, or digitally downloaded book, something of that nature). A good affiliate marketing program does not involve any kind of MLM or Ponzi scheme type set up and is based on moving products to the buying public. When the product sells, you get paid a commission.

When you get right down to it, affiliate marketing involves two things.

The first is that you're pre-selling potential customers on the product. We will explore how to do this in detail later, but you're going to create feedback or websites or email campaigns that gently persuade people that the product is right for them. Of course, it's not going to work all the time or even a large percentage of the time. But all you need to do is get some of the people you are coming in contact with, whether it's through a blog, Facebook, or Instagram – to be interested in the product. For some products, it's going to be easy, and there are ways to tap into people who are online already looking for the products you're selling. Other times it's going to take a little more work, but the rewards may be outsized

Have you ever stopped to consider just how online shopping works? It may seem obvious to you, but when you buy a product online, there are generally four ways in which a seller can deliver this product to your doorstep.

They ship the product to you themselves. In this instance, the seller has the product on hand, packages it themselves, and ships it to your address. This is probably the most obvious method for sellers to utilize, but it necessarily the best for all entrepreneurs.

It is a digital product, and there's no shipping required. This is a wonderful situation for an entrepreneur attempting to make sales online, but unless you're in the digital publishing or software business, there's a good chance this won't apply to you.

The seller originally purchased the product, but has a third-party fulfillment service that ships their goods. This is a growing trend. As space limitations and time limitations make it difficult for small teams (or even sole proprietors) to handle a large amount of shipping and handling on top of their other business requirements, services like Fulfillment by Amazon handle the process of shipping goods as they are sold. The seller still buys the product, so the investment in terms of cost is actually higher than shipping on your own, but often the time freed allows for scaling the business and working on finding new products and working on marketing rather than the labor of getting a package to a customer.

The seller lists a product they have not bought, and a supplier ships the product to the consumer when a sale is made. This is known as drop-shipping, and the initial investment on the part of the seller is much less than traditional sales. However, with dropshipping come additional costs for products and often additional fees, meaning lower profit margins per sale. However, because the initial investment is mostly time, this means that more risks can be taken on a large range of products, and scaling the business can begin

almost immediately, rather than when funds allow for it. This makes dropshipping one of the premier methods for those getting started.

While dropshipping isn't by any means the only way to reach a six- figure e-commerce goal, it is perhaps the least stressful and the most open ended. For this reason, many of us in the e-commerce field begin here even if we eventually branch out into other forms of sales as well. For those of us that prefer to put in the time rather than the cost, such as having a limited budget to start with, it is perhaps the best possible method of becoming a successful e-commerce entrepreneur.

Dropshipping is becoming an increasingly common way to do business online, taking the fundamentals of e-commerce but simply adding a middleman to take care of the shipping and supply. There is huge potential to make an impressive income if you remain focused and determined while keeping on top of managing your business. While you may not be spending time packing and sending orders, there is still plenty of work to do, though you will be mainly focused on sales and marketing to grow and expand your operations.

Your customer does not see you. You are a ghost in the entire operation. Every step of this dropshipping process can be done with just a laptop and a Wi-Fi connection. There is huge potential when it comes to this lucrative business model. Firstly, you do not have to stock any products nor pay for product storage. Secondly, you will only pay for the product after your customer has paid for it. You are using part of your customer's money to pay for the product. The remaining amount will be your profit of course. Hence there is zero capital risk involved in the entire operation. Talk about a risk-free investment. However, like all businesses, your time and effort are required to make this a success.

These days, a lot of emphasis on being placed on the value of being able to work from home and earn money through your computer. For many, online marketing and e-commerce is a powerful opportunity to step out of financial ruin and into a state of financial freedom, with the added benefit of time freedom as well. With the way the economy seems to be going, I suspect that one day everyone will have some form of involvement in e-commerce as a way to subsidize or supplement their income, if not replace their income altogether.

You have likely seen the stories about people who decide to try e-commerce, only to realize that they tapped into a massive revenue stream that has earned those thousands, if not millions, of dollars every single year. From bloggers who have leveraged their websites for an income to individuals who have stepped onto platforms like Amazon, it seems like many have a form of "rags to riches" story that has left the rest of the world in awe. For many, it also seems like a deal that is simply too good to be true, and that they should not even bother trying because there is no way it could possibly work for them.

To those people, I say do your research.

E-commerce is a thriving powerhouse that continues to turn everyday people into individuals who are earning massive amounts of wealth and changing the future of their lives forever. There is no time like the present to get started, which is why I am so excited that you are here right now learning how to navigate the world of Amazon FBA!

Getting started as soon as possible is key in positioning yourself into the world of e-commerce and earning a piece of the pie for yourself. When you choose to get started with e-commerce, the moment you make the leap you set up the opportunity for your entire future to change. You not only open yourself up to create financial freedom

for yourself, but you also set yourself up to receive many other benefits that come with financial freedom being earned through a strategy like e-commerce. For example, you create the opportunity for you to work from anywhere you desire, spend your days doing anything you wish to do, and design the lifestyle that you desire to have for yourself right down to the very last detail. Countless benefits come from the financial freedom and time freedom that you will earn for yourself through launching and managing a successful Amazon FBA business.

The best part is: this business can be built out in a highly passive manner, too. Many people think that you have to have a lot of time and energy to pour into launching an online business, or any business for that matter, in order to see it succeed. However, based on the nature of Amazon FBA and how this program works, you actually step into a form of e-commerce that is easier and more passive than virtually any other form of e-commerce out there. Through this platform, all you have to do is source products, place them for sale, and advertise them to your audience of individuals who are ready to purchase the products from you. Then, all you have to do is let Amazon employees manage the process of actually shipping your products to your customers, while you keep products in stock and source new products to grow your business with.

The concept of Amazon FBA is simple, which is exactly what makes it an incredible business opportunity for those who are new to e-commerce. Instead of having to manage everything from web development to inventory management, shipping and everything else, you simply have to manage marketing while making sure that everything stays in stock. This makes your role in the business wildly easy, meaning that you can grow your Amazon FBA business as a side business, or grow it and let the income sustain your freedom-based lifestyle.

In Amazon FBA, we are going to discuss everything you need to know about Amazon FBA, including what it is and how to get started with this business model. By the end of this book, you will be able to confidently design your own Amazon FBA business and grow it to massive success in minimal timing. Through this, you are

going to be able to transform your own finances and open yourself up to the opportunity of living your best possible lifestyle.

If you are ready to begin learning the ways of Amazon FBA and preparing to launch your own Amazon FBA business, it is time to begin. Please, enjoy the process. You are about to make some massive, life-changing moves in the coming weeks!

CHAPTER 1 YOUTUBE MARKETING AND ADVERTISING

Over the years, YouTube became synonymous with opportunities to put your brand in evidence, because it is possible that you appear before your audience and that you have close relationships with content that stimulates interactivity.

Seeing that it is the most popular video platform in the world and the second most used search site on the planet, being present there is crucial for your company. On the other hand, YouTube is directly linked to Google, which can contribute to improve the positioning of your site in web searches.

If you want to make videos and spread them online, you need to have a good planning and invest in some particularities, such as the quality of your materials. Today, with so much content available on the internet, it is important to make investments so you can offer some quality.

Data behind the YouTube monster There are more than one billion users Every day hundreds of millions of hours are seen and billions of reproductions are generated

300 hours of video are uploaded every minute 50% of the reproductions are from mobiles
YouTube is available in 75 countries and 61 languages

There are more than 1 million advertisers (most are small businesses)

YouTube video marketing work is increasingly essential for a successful strategy. In the end, the contents of this type have a high potential to transmit information and contribute to the dissemination of products and services.

Although the content is the king on the web, it is very important that you worry about the most technical aspects, such as a study, which is one of the most appropriate solutions to help you save money with production and also have more dynamic processes and less bureaucratic

Then, before worrying about the equipment and all other things, the first step is to find a suitable place to set up the studio to record your videos, in order to meet your needs in terms of structure and equipment.

That way, later we will highlight the 3 main steps for you to have your own study. Look!

The Space

Remember that the studio needs to have enough space for you to record your videos, for the equipment, the actors and the technical team. A place that is small can be very bad for the quality of the videos produced and also cause some kind of accident since the production equipment is fragile and can be easily damaged

Acoustics

Always look for places that are as distant as possible from noise. Always privileges the isolation of any type of sound that may hinder the recording. Another recommendation to protect you from noise is through investments in expanded polystyrene plates or foams, which can be placed on windows and doors. On the other hand, egg maps are also efficient to make the acoustics of the environment better and you can place them above the foams.

Lighting and Colors

If you were to use a closed room as a study, you should invest in lighting. Therefore, never forget that a poorly lit or shadowy scene can make your production ruined.

So, if you cannot count on natural light, which is very difficult, pay attention to illuminate the environment in the best possible way.

Another issue that needs attention is the color of the environment you will use. In the end, depending on the paint and the color used on the wall, the light can be reflected with color and make your whole scene look bad.

Therefore, you should give preference to opaque paints, which absorb light instead of reflecting it. On the other hand, if you use a wall layer as the background of the images, choose the most neutral colors that do not cause much interference, in case they are reflected on products or people.

White ends up being an excellent option and, in case you want, you can always decorate the walls with paintings, clocks or elements that have to do with the content. If you have the technical knowledge and want to produce more professional videos, it is worth investing in a chroma-key.

Finally, it is worth remembering that you must take care of the organization of the stage as a whole, that is, always have a beautiful and clean environment. This will bring a lot of credibility to the

videos and will ensure you a number of subscribers on YouTube and, consequently, a participatory and connected audience.

Equipment Choice

The quality of videos is one of the essential factors for you to succeed in the YouTube strategy The good news is that there are investments for all budgets. You can record with a more solid camera and even with your smartphone.

It is important to invest in audio quality and good lighting, which will make a leap in the quality of your recordings. Next, we will highlight some equipment for image, audio and lighting. Look!

Image

When opting for cameras, there are numerous models and prices. Regardless of whether you choose a smartphone, a webcam or a more compact camera, what is really worth is the budget. Then, study the possibilities:

tight budget: in case you have a cell phone with a good camera, preferably in Full HD, you will know that you have material that has advanced technology. A problem with the cell phone is the few focus adjustment options, but it is perfectly possible to record excellent videos for YouTube with the phone, duly attached to a tripod;

medium budget: the most compact cameras, depending on the model, are worse than many more recent cell phones. Because of that, it is very important that you pay attention and choose those that have a value similar to the input DSLR cameras;

Looser budget: DSLR cameras are the best bets for you to have optimal video quality. If you want something more practical, bet on that type of camera. But there are some simpler models within that category, such as the Canon T5 and Nikon D3200.

Audio

Audio is very important for recording quality videos. In the case of camera audio, it ends up being damaged by the environment, so the microphone ends up being necessary. In that case, pay attention to the possibilities:

tight budget: your smartphone probably has a microphone embedded in the hearing aid. It is not the most perfect scenario, but you can record your voice separately on the cell phone that way. Thus, you hide the hearing aid in the shirt and hold the microphone in the neck. The sound may not be so perfect, but it will probably be cleaner than the camera sound.

Medium budget: you have the option of investing in a lapel microphone with a connector that is serious in the smartphone. Recording with a lapel microphone, the sound quality of your video will be much better and your audio will be clear to your audience.

Looser budget: in case you record alone, invest in a lapel microphone and a digital recorder. You can find some kit options with good recorder microphones. Unquestionably, the result will be much better.

Illumination

Good lighting is also essential to get your viewers to follow your videos from beginning to end. Although natural light works perfectly for different videos, you can also invest in some types of equipment, such as a panel of LED lights, which can be installed directly on the camera.

Although you can make more solid investments, as in the LimoStudio kit, which creates light and diffuse Illuminations, or in a Neewer Camera, a ring light, which is circular and can be installed in the camera.

Use YouTube Video Techniques in Your Favor

So that the work you present on YouTube has an excellent level of quality, you can use some filming techniques, which are essential to do a differentiated and successful work. Below, we highlight recommendations that may be indispensable for your strategy. Let's go to them:

lighting: a well-lit video is vital for your content to be viewed in a completely comfortable way by the viewers, since it prevents data, information and some places from being hidden;

animations: animations offer endless possibilities for you to create your videos. They give dynamism to your content and can be another attraction for people to really be attentive to your ideas;

narration: some more complex concepts can become a very difficult task to express. Therefore, a more personal narrative can make all the difference when explaining some ideas;

music: choosing a piece of music that transmits the desired emotions is an excellent way to give strength to the contents of the videos ;

humor: using humor is another way of fixing the public's attention in a general way, but you must do that in a very timely manner and avoid excessive informality;

graphics: listing the fruits on the performance of a company in the course of the video can become somewhat boring, but through the use of infographics it is possible to make the understanding of information easier, in addition to avoiding reading the numbers;

emotion: telling exciting stories are great ways to pass the company's message to the public and can make a connection with customers established. On the other hand, it is worth remembering that exciting videos sell more;

Duration: choosing how long a video will last is a very important technique since it is essential to find a balance between the speed in which ideas are expressed and the period in which the user will be attentive to the video;

colors and filters: using colors and image filters is essential to give more depth to the messages and these can be used both in more comparative videos, as in others with more educational character;

Company history: telling a brief history of the company and its processes so far is an essential technique to value all the progress achieved. On the other hand, it reinforces the identity and image of the brand.

Ensure you use content that is really relevant to your audience. The contents must solve the problems of your audience and to help you in this task we will highlight 9 content ideas for YouTube. Look!

1. Explanatory Videos

   People really like video tutorials, in which things are explained in detail. Making videos that clarify people's doubts is a great way to have many views and participation.

2. Promotional Videos

   It is necessary to pay attention to the promotions of products and services that your audience has an interest in. Based on this, you can create content for some promotions you are doing. Remember that everyone likes a promotion and you can exploit that strategy in a timely manner.

3. Vlogs

   People love to know details of the racks in people's lives. Therefore, if it were something that suits your business, you can make more informal videos, telling about the content you learned, events you participated in, among other issues.

4. Recommendations
   People like to receive recommendations of all types. Therefore, if you have any ideas or are experts in some subjects, make videos indicating ideas that will certainly help your audience.

5. Make Webinars

Webinars are live videos in which you can give a class or a dissertation. Its duration usually varies and depends a lot on the subject and the type of audience you want to reach. It is an excellent way to establish closer relationships with potential consumers and create your authority in the market.

Audio Marketing: the evolution of content

Undoubtedly, audio is the type of multimedia that can best adapt to the routine: even with the existence of other content distribution formats, it lost its importance.

Read more "

6. Customer Stories

You can promote some videos by telling success stories of some clients. Remember that people connect more easily with other people than with brands.

7. Videos on How to Do

Many people go to the internet to solve their problems. From the moment you create videos teaching people to do things, you will naturally build a good audience.

8. Personal Videos

People like to know about experiences. Therefore, if you have any interesting personal history that refers to the professional context, you can exploit that in the videos and generate very identification with your audience.

9. Motivational Videos

Motivational videos are also an excellent idea for you to identify with your audience and make him participate with your brand.

Configure the YouTube Channel

In case you have finished creating a YouTube channel, we will give you essential recommendations for you to stand out. Follow, below, some channel configuration recommendations:

1. Add channel art and profile picture

    It is very important that you add an art for the channel and a profile picture to have a visual identity that is easily recognized by your audience. For the profile (or avatar), it is interesting that you have a logo and for the art (or cover photo) you can use images that

    establish a synergy of your work with what you will address in your channel.

2. Add a description and the client of your other digital platforms

    To describe your business, it is interesting to tell a little about your story and your proposal on YouTube. It is worth presenting, for example, your mission, vision and values. It is also an excellent opportunity to add links from other platforms, such as Facebook, Instagram and Twitter. For that, you need to go to the settings and enable the option "Customize the layout of your channel".

3. Upload videos

    To upload a video on YouTube, you just need to click on the arrow icon, which is at the top edge, to the right of the screen.

Next, the tab will appear to upload the video. You have the option to select several videos or, if not, you can upload one at a time.

An important recommendation is that, at the time of uploading, you should place the videos in the private option. That way, you can edit it before it is released to the public. After having everything correct, you can put the video as public.

4. Understand the differences between public, unlisted and private

On YouTube, there is a possibility that you configure the privacy of videos. There are three options and each of them has some peculiarities:

Private: When you select this option, videos cannot be viewed by the channel owner. It is recommended to place it in private when the video is not yet finished or when you wish that no one else has access to its content;

Not listed: through this option, your video can only be seen by the people you want, that is, the general public will not be able to access. In that case, the channel owner sends the video link to the people he wants to see.

Public: This option allows the video to be open on your channel and viewed by anyone who searches

Create a check-list

To be successful with your YouTube video strategy, it is very interesting that you have a check-list to highlight all the steps of your videos. In the first moment, you can check your steps in four situations:

1. Preproduction

At this stage, you need to be aware of issues such as duration, format, quantity of videos and content management. Here, it is also the ideal time for you to write a video script, fully aligned with the needs and motivations of your audience.

2. Production

Some content corrections will also be made because many times what was put on paper is not very good in the video. On the other hand, in this stage, the care related to the place of the recording, the formats and the angles also correspond so that everything goes perfectly.

3. Post-production

At this stage, the entire video must be evaluated before being released by means of opinion tests between the teams and the management of the company.

4. Disclosure

This is one of the most important stages for professionals involved in the video marketing strategy for YouTube. After all, remember that, with good content in hand, the possibilities of a video are unlimited.

In this case, it is worth the disclosure on the site itself in social networks in e-mail marketing, so that you guarantee the effective opening rate and, mainly, a greater conversion concerning other types of format.

In addition to evaluating each of these stages, it is essential that you are attentive to the SEO strategy for YouTube, so that your video

can appear well positioned on Google. To stand out, it is necessary to invest in the following techniques:

always use keywords in the title;

know all the tools of YouTube and learn how to exploit them;

effectively describe your video and learn to use tags;

share it on social networks, sites and wherever you can; use calls for action (CTAs) in videos.

CHAPTER 2 CONTENTS THAT GO VIRAL

I'll work with the example of my hemp business, and the customer persona is: people that love hemp but do not know where to get it from.

These are the innovators- the kind of people that have been waiting all their lives to buy hemp from a reputable online store.

So, as I fill out a customer persona worksheet, like the one you can find in the resources page at the very end of this book, this is what some of my answers look like:

Background:

Job: Anything.

Career Path/industry: Anything. Company:

Family: Have siblings.

Education: University (degree and student debt). Generally, how do we relate to them?

What're their values: They like Hemp, do they not smoke it. They want to legalize it, like medical marijuana but not need it themselves. They would use Hemp and appreciate it. They are fanboys and will go crazy for anything even remotely Hemp. Show off their love of Hemp.

What's important to them? Access to new ideas and new products. Access to Hemp products and stuff that is made from their favorite thing.

They want to (increase business, dress in hemp, raise awareness of hemp): Use Hemp and raise its awareness. Make other people know that it exists and that it is awesome.

What are they committed to: Raising awareness of hemp, using alternatives stuff.

Pain Points - things they may also Google for to find a solution for:

Fear: When Hemp legislation loses a ballet. When something bad is said about it. When they hear reports about how bad it is in the media, or when they hear other people badmouthing it.

Lack: well-researched Information to make a coherent defense of hemp.

Desire: To hear about success stories in places like Colorado where because of Hemp legalization taxes have gone up and crime has gone down.

Want: A place to get Hemp, information to share with others in Hemp's defense. More evidence that Hemp is safe. More evidence that Marijuana is not the same as Hemp. And ways to expose the biased media/politicians against Hemp.

Need: More tools and evidence.

Obstacles: A lot of articles out there are from non-Hemp dedicated sources. How can we create ideas about / appeal to their sense of...

A sense of delight: When there is a new Hemp product. When it is legalized somewhere. When an opposed to hemp is proven wrong. When a new factory opens up. Hearing about a new industry using it. New innovations that use Hemp.

Adventure:

Amusement (Humor):

Appeal to their sense of learning: To learn as much as they can about Hemp.

Astonished:

Awe (surprise, unexpectedness or mystery): Contextual (a sense of drama/movement)

Creativity: Creative uses of Hemp as furniture. Credibility:
Curiosity (a knowledge gap):

Delighted:
Emotion:
Environment:

Remember, you don't need to answer all of the questions, but enough to get a rounded view of whom it is you want to work with and attract to your business. But remember: the more you answer and fill in, the more ideas you can generate later on.

Then we begin to ask 'why is it important?' on the major topics, thus breaking down different answers in the attempt to create content that'll attract customers to the business.

As I began to breakdown the customer's beliefs and intentions to an emotional level, thus we could come up with a variety of different content to attract them.

Pleasant Surprise:

When they learn about different products that can be made of Hemp.
When they learn about different online stores that sell hemp things.

When we share with them big/popular natural/organic stores in their area.

Self Esteem:

If/When we find and share with them any research that connects hemp with a healthier/happier life.

How hemp has changed lives and industries around the world, and how those same benefits can be applied to them.

Sense of Magic:

Explaining how these simple chemicals can revolutionize lives and industries.

How this single plan has saved lives through medicine. Curiosity: Explaining why Hemp was banned in the first place. How it is we can reverse those laws.

The effects of the war on drugs in everyday peoples' lives.

So, then let's take a few of these and break them down. I'll start with the first one 'Pleasant Surprise', and "When they learn about different products that can be made of Hemp".

So, why is this important to them?

Because he wants to know where the stores are.

When he knows where they are, he can get certain kinds of products.
When he knows where they are, he can incorporate them into his routine.
Let's take the first point: Because he wants to know where the stores are.

Why is that important?

So, he can then begin shopping there.
He is a willing customer that wants to buy hemp-related products. Then you could ask once more:
So, he can then start using hemp in his life. Because he wants to support local hemp businesses.
When you understand your customers and begin understating why they want what they want, then you can begin to create content that is perfect

for them. Content that is likely to seek out, consume, see you as an expert, begin to trust you and begin to buy from you

From examples just mentioned, here are some ways that I could create content just for him:

A list of stores that sell hemp in the X local area.

What hemp products should be part of your daily route and why. Why support local hemp and organic stores.

What kind of stores are the best for product X. Or, which online stores specialize in selling X kind of Hemp products.

These will either be in the form of a book, infographic, YouTube video, Facebook video, blog, etc. The form it is delivered depends on the complexity and versatility of the idea.

You want to deliver the information to them in a way that they can consume relative to the complexity of the subject. In this case either an infographic or a blog that simply lists the places.

The more of these kinds of content you have, the more you can attract the perfect kinds of customers.

CHAPTER 3 TIKTOK MARKETING AND ADVERTISING

Now you can't really make money off the videos on TikTok, but you can make money off the live feature on TikTok. With the live feature, you can get people to donate. However, you can only use the live feature if you've over 1000 fans.

So now that you know how to use the TikTok platform. TikTok is an undervalued social media and is already pretty fast. It's just like a snap chat. It's already halfway to Snapchat. You can use TikTok to start making money on YouTube by doing compilations from your TikTok account. You can make compilations of TikTok on YouTube like TikTok memes, TikTok compilations that make your day a little better. This is not the copy and paste video strategy that you see everywhere on YouTube. Instead, you're good to be getting the videos yourself from TikTok. You can make anywhere from $6k to $100k every month just by doing some compilations on YouTube from TikTok.

How to Make Real Money with TikTok

Despite the average age of users on the platform, the platform can still be a great way to make money. You can just post ads on the app and have people impulsive buy from your shop, but remember, the kids don't have credit cards, they can't go to the app and purchase something. They'll probably have to go to their parents to get their parent's credit card, their parents have to approve the website, and your product before the kids will buy. However, there are simpler ways to make money through the app.

Get Big with It

 The first method is to create videos on the app and try to get big with it. It's a fairly new app, and there are not enough seasoned creators to compete with. If you go out there and make it big on TikTok, you want to be able to transfer your audience on other platforms as soon as you can and as heavily as you can. We saw this happened during the days of Vine. Some people used the app to grow a huge following on there, and they were able to transfer that following into Instagram and YouTube. However, if those people were stuck to doing vines, then their career would have ended as soon as Vine ended, but instead, they transferred their audience to YouTube, and now they are some of the biggest creators on YouTube. So, if you get big on a trendy app like TikTok, you should transfer your audience as soon as possible; because if you don't, then your career is going to die as soon as the success of the app decreases. So, if your audience is on TikTok and you want to grow a YouTube channel, then it's easier to first grow on TikTok and then transfer your audience to YouTube.

TikTok Compilations on YouTube

It's mind-blowing the amount of money that people are making using this method. The good thing with YouTube is that when you upload a video on YouTube, and you pass a certain number of subscribers and watched hours, then you'll be able to connect your channel with something called Google AdSense. AdSense start playing advertisements on your videos even before people click on

the play button, and you earn a percentage of the advertisement that is being played on it.

So, you're basically taking compilation videos from TikTok and posting it on YouTube. When Vine was existing, many channels were not doing this until Vine disappeared, and those channels didn't have any content to post again on their YouTube channel. So TikTok is the new version of Vine. If you go to YouTube and search for TikTok compilations, you'll see videos with over 230 million views on YouTube achieved in six months. The views on these compilation videos are insane and out of this world. So, these people making TikTok videos on YouTube get paid based on CPM, Which is how much you get paid per 100 views, and it varies from channel to channel depending on the content that you're making. If you're making high-quality education videos, then you'll have a higher CPM compared to someone that's making prank videos.

The average CPM on compilation videos will be about $1.5. So, on the videos that are making 230 million views, all you need to do is to take that

230 million views divide by 1000 and multiply that by

$1.5 to get the amount of money that they are making. So, if you do the calculation, you'll get $342,000 as of the money that they made in six months. There is also a video on TikTok compilations that had about 93 million views in 8 months, so to get the amount of money that they are making, all you have to do is to take that 93 million, divide it by 1000 and then multiply it by $1.5 to get over

$139,500. There is also another YouTube channel that got around 46 million views in the last 30 days, so if you do the math, you'll see that the channel owner made about $69,000 in the last 30 days, which means the channel is making about $70,000 a month from reposting TikTok compilations. But here is the catch, that channel has been uploading videos constantly. The more they upload, the more views they're able to get, and the more money they make. If you stroll through the TikTok videos, you'll see that they're getting hundreds of millions of views. The reason why these videos are getting a lot of views is that they are made up of little videos, so even if you've got the attention of a goldfish, you'll definitely want to watch through because you'll see a new video every 10 seconds. So, people are clicking on them and watching them through, which

implies that the number of watched hours achieved through these videos is amazing, which is gold for the YouTube algorithm. Most of the videos are clickbait, but people are hardly going to click off the videos as they would in other videos, because even though if they have a short attention span, they're going to keep watching since new videos are popping up every 10 seconds. And once YouTube has seen that people are clicking on the videos and spending a lot of time on their website, then they are going to recommend those videos to other people.

Doing the Research for Your Next Compilation

This strategy involves you to take other videos, to cut them down and put them together to make your own videos. And guess what? You don't even have to show your face if you don't want to. You can create a YouTube channel and start making money just by creating TikTok videos. YouTube doesn't care about subscribers; they only care about views. So, the more videos you can create the better. The best part of this, is that you don't even have to create or film these videos yourself. All you're going to do is to compile a list of TikTok videos and then throw a bunch of ads on them. It's that simple. A lot of people are already using this strategy; you can go on social blade to confirm that. On social Blade, you can search for TikTok videos and then check how much per day those guys creating those TikTok videos are making. Now, in case you're wondering how the site knows how much those guys are making; it's pretty simple to know for sure! YouTube pays their influencers based on CPM, which is the cost per 1000 views. You'll be able to see the views that those guys creating those TikTok compilations are making from the social blade site, and all you have to do is the math to find out how much they are making every day. For example, if you can create a video that hit up to 7 million views (which is possible!), then you'll make $ 32,000. If you think this number is impossible to make, then you need to visit the social blade site to see the insane amount of views that those guys are achieving on their videos and how much those guys are making by just posting those videos.

Creating the Compilations

To get started, go to the TikTok app, and then look for a video on TikTok. Click on a video and then click on save video, and it'll save the video under your gallery. Then go to Google Play and download the TikTok video downloader; after doing that, open the app, minimize it, go to your TikTok app, click on the share button, copy the link and download the TikTok from there. Once you've got the video on your phone, email it to yourself and download it on your computer. Now open up a video editing software. VSDC is a good video editing software that you can easily use. You can also use Sony Vegas, whichever video editing software you use it's perfectly fine. So, you're going to open the video editing software. In this case, we are using VSDC. Now go to whatever folder that you saved the videos in, click on it to open it up. So, open up the video editing software, create a project and name it TikTok compilations videos. Now drag and drop all your videos. You're going to shorten the video to make it 3 or 6 seconds long. Find the interesting part of the video and squish that part until it fits under 6 seconds, make sure that the part you are cutting out is really interesting. Or you can actually shorten the front part of the video and then extend the back part of it to make it 6 seconds long. Once you get the interesting part of all the videos, you can then go ahead and merge them together. In the end, you're going to have a compilation of different videos that are just about 6 seconds each. Every single video of TikTok works well in retaining the viewers' attention on YouTube. You can choose to do a compilation video of girls; you can also do compilation videos of dancers or the funniest memes on TikTok. You can start by making 5-minute long compilation videos of TikTok and then later increase the compilation videos to 10 minutes. Once you start gaining traction on the YouTube platform, you can start adding ads into the video and monetizing your video to make money. Once you're done creating your video, export it, go on YouTube and create a YouTube channel. You can name your channel something like TikTok best or TikTok entertainment, and then add those videos on your channel every single day. If you're consistent with, sooner or later your views will definitely start to grow, and you'll start to get an insane amount of views. People are using this strategy and getting 2000 subscribers every single day

with millions of views. Those people are earning over 200-300 Dollars every day or at least something within that range.

While creating these videos, make sure that you use the same type of title. The only thing that you should change is the thumbnails. A good thumbnail will be able to get you many views. One way to create a good thumbnail is to go to other popular and successful TikTok compilation YouTubers to see and compare all their thumbnails that got a lot of views and see how you can make better thumbnails, not by copying them, but by taking a cue to make better thumbnails than theirs. If you see that a TikTok compilations YouTuber made a challenge on one of his videos, and it got a lot of views, then do the same on yours. Thumbnails are very important on YouTube because of something called CTR, which is the click- through rate. The average click-through rate is around 2-4%, so you want to make sure that you're getting a good click-through rate for your videos. If your CTR is over 10%, then that's a good sign that your video is going to go viral. Normally, you want your videos to enter the suggested area of the popular videos so that YouTube can help you promote your videos alongside with other videos that are going viral.

Getting Views from the Search Results

On YouTube, you can actually get views from people that are searching for a particular keyword on the platform. The first thing that you should do is to go to the YouTube search bar and type in the keyword that you want to rank for. As you type in the keyword, you'll also see other keywords that you can use in conjunction with the one that you just typed. The search bar on YouTube is cool because it gives you what people are searching for so that you can rank your videos based on what people are searching for. So, you can go viral by looking for the things that are already reigning on YouTube. Also, the targeting that you use on YouTube is going to play a huge roll in whether your video will go viral or not. When you have a good title, a good thumbnail, and a good text, you'll definitely start ranking on YouTube. That is how you make your videos go viral. Use your keywords in the text of your titles. Use the keywords in your tags and descriptions too. Even when you're giving credit, use the keywords there. If you use the keywords so

many times in your video, YouTube will know that your video is about that keyword. Once you start getting more watched hours on your videos; YouTube will push your videos up the algorithm. However, You also need to insert a niche into your TikTok video, to give people an overview of what your videos are about. For example, you can choose to create funny TikTok video compilations and search for keywords like "I baked you a pie". This means that your keywords will change on every video, the same thing applies to the tags and description, but your TikTok niche will remain the same. Therefore, if you're creating a video on "I baked you a pie," you can use the keywords: "I baked you a pie meme", "I baked you pie lyrics", "I baked you a full pie song", "I baked you a pie TikTok", "I baked you a pie distorted". Just go to the search bar on YouTube and type the keyword "I baked you a pie", or "I baked you a pie TikTok", and you'll see so many keywords recommendations come up. YouTube allows you to create up to a 500 character-based text. Creating a good description, with a good thumbnail, and some keywords will make your videos rank well on the YouTube platform

CHAPTER 4 LINKEDIN MARKETING AND ADVERTISING

With more than 562 million members from all over the world, LinkedIn is the largest and most popular professional network. If you want to develop your relationships and grow your network, it is an absolute must for your company to be involved on LinkedIn. It is, after all, the lead generation's largest social network.

LinkedIn, being a website that links companies and experts, requires a unique marketing strategy, of course. The law here is the word of mouth. It's not about whom you know, but whom, through the people you know, you can connect with. But it won't turn out to be a successful marketing campaign to sell your brand through your obsolete personal page. Read on to see how your winning marketing strategy can be developed (and implemented) to get you to the top on LinkedIn.

Setting Up Your LinkedIn Company Page

You need a full-blown business profile for marketing your brand on LinkedIn. The business page is a professional way to let members of LinkedIn know about your name, your products, your organization and the job opportunities provided by your company.

Although the business websites were mainly used as HR landing pages, this website now offers a great opportunity to raise awareness of the brand and market your services to potential clients.

You need an active personal profile on LinkedIn first to set up a company website. If you have one, just follow the next steps to build your company's website.

Add your company

Type your company name and create a URL to help people find your website. Note that later you won't be able to change the URL, so make sure you choose wisely. Then check the checkbox to check that you are the company's official representative and click' Launch Account.'

The shell will be created automatically. Only press the 'Get Started' button to start creating your website.

Add your image

Import your logo (recommended 300x 300 pixels) as your profile image and add a cover image (preferably 1536x 768 px) to give an insight into what your business is about. Keep in mind that logos businesses have more traffic, so don't be tempted to miss this phase.

You have 20 specialties to add. Think of them as keywords advertisements that can help people discover their business on LinkedIn, so be sure to reflect the business ' power and knowledge here.

- Company details

  Here you enter the location of your company, the URL of your website, your industry, the size and form of your product, as well as other important details identifying your company.

- Publish the page

  Tap ' Publish' to go online. It is best to see what the business page looks like when other people press on it before you start. Tap ' Member Window' to try it out. If the look of your page is not satisfied, go to' Manage Page' and make some modifications.

- Page Administrators

  If you're not planning to run your LinkedIn Company page alone, you'll need to select the people you can administer the page.

  Tap on the 'Me' button at the top of your screen to add more staff. Go to 'Manage', and then select your Company Page. There, pick the 'Admin Tools' option for 'Web Admins'. Enter the name of the users you want to view the list.

  Note: To pick them as admins, you must already be linked to these individuals on LinkedIn.

Only having a business website doesn't mean you're going to get the right connections. You also need to have a good marketing plan for LinkedIn, just like any other site. Here's what you can do to improve your chances of success:

Create a Showcase Page

Showcase pages are the perfect way to display a particular part of your company you're most proud of. This is a great opportunity to put your best product in the spotlight and attract potential customers.

The view pages act as some kind of subdomains for your business website and having one can really make a difference because members on LinkedIn can also visit them individually if they are specifically interested in a particular product or service. You can have pages up to view.

Tap the' Me ' button to build one, then pick your Company Page under' Manage.' Then go to' Admin Tools'—' Create a page for a showcase.'

Have Your Employees Connected

Your employees are your biggest advocates on LinkedIn. Having them as followers means you have access to their networks and connections, which can increase your reach significantly and bring more traffic to your company page. Encourage your employees to be connected to your company page to raise awareness of the brand.

Keep Followers Informed

The easiest way to boost your market is to be happy with the one you have. Make sure you write valuable content on your business on a regular basis, such as blogs, blog posts or other updates. Even, if you can conceive of a worthwhile external post for your fans, do not hesitate to publish it as well.

Choose LinkedIn Groups

LinkedIn Groups provide you with a perfect way to connect with people in your immediate circle from your profession. Active in a LinkedIn Community and engaged in conversations will lead to more visits to your site.

Would you like to find a group that suits your goal? With the 'Group Discover' option, you can check out some suggestions for LinkedIn, or just use the search bar if you know what you're looking for.

Go Global

If you have clients in some countries where English is not the official language, then you may want to consider adding a summary in other languages of your product. Don't worry, for that reason you don't have to find a translator. LinkedIn offers multi-language tools for you to take care of this.

Publish at the Right Times

Like the plans for your other sites, you also need to schedule your LinkedIn posting. Data from LinkedIn says the best time to post material on LinkedIn is in the morning and after business hours. This is when people are most involved, so you may want to take advantage of this knowledge and then plan your message.

If you want to direct your message to other practitioners, whether CEOs or influencers, you should definitely take advantage of ads on LinkedIn. You will start with the next steps after you decide what you want to promote and who is your target audience.

- Your 'Campaign Manager' Account

    This is a tool that gives you the easiest way to manage and automate your advertising. However, this app provides some useful tools to show the output of your ads, so it's an added bonus.

- Choose the Type of Your Ad

    Next, the type of ad you want to advertise must be selected. Three options are available:

- Sponsored InMail

- Sponsored content

- Text Ad

    With all three forms, you can also build your advertisement to ensure maximum coverage.

    Once you choose the ad form, enter your campaign name, select the language of your target audience, and select the call-to-action feature, which is only available for the Sponsored-Content advertisements.

- Create the Ad

    The best thing about the Campaign Manager is to guide you

through the production steps, giving advice and guidance along the way.

Follow the steps choosing the most appropriate choices for your target.

- Target the Ad

  Make sure your ad is aimed at the right people at this point. You may state such requirements such as location, names of classes, company names, degree, job title, class, age, years of experience, qualifications, etc. Make sure that you save your qualifications so that the next time you want to advertise on LinkedIn you can speed things up.

- Set the Budget and Schedule

  There are three options you can pay for ads:

- Cost per click (CPC)

- Cost per impression (CPM)–for user display messages

  - Cost per send–for supported InMail advertising (here you only pay for receiving messages)

  For the CPM and CPS alternative, you are allowed to set a maximum daily budget you are willing to spend and a bid price. Just plan the beginning and end date and time for the ad after that, and you're done.

Is Your Marketing Strategy Working?

When you take your stats from another social media platform, the real picture of your LinkedIn success is probably missing. Checking out the built-in analytics tool on LinkedIn is the best way to check whether your marketing strategy works.

Go to the top of your screen toolbar fount and press the' Analytics' tab. You can see that there are three options available:

• Visitors-This is where data is stored on the people visiting your website. Here you can see a general overview of page views, user stats, you can separate data from a certain time and date, see data

from different sites on your site, and see detailed information about users visiting your page (job feature, venue, sector, etc.)

• Feedback–here you can find information about the content you post. Such indicators of communication include views, downloads, shares, comments, taps, etc.

CHAPTER 5 SNAPCHAT AND PINTEREST

Snapchat

Among the new online life stage alternatives, one of the quickest developing is Snapchat, so advertisers consequently accept they should take their bit of that possibly worthwhile pie.

Snap, Inc., is Snapchat's parent organization, and holds a current market valuation of around $25 billion. While chipping away at profiting by this may appear to be an easy decision, this internet- based life stage isn't ideal for each brand.

Snapchat reports aggressive client commitment contrasted with other internet-based life stages. A great many people check online life applications consistently, in some cases a few times each day. Clients check Snapchat multiple times every day by and large, and over 2.5 billion snaps make a trip through the system to more than 150 million clients consistently. Indeed, over 45% of every one of the 18-to 55-year-olds in the United States utilize Snapchat. In the event that you need to take advantage of this possibly tremendous achievement, you should painstakingly think about how to use Snapchat viably for your image.

Is Your Brand Compatible with Snapchat?

Snapchat enables clients to send photographs and brief recordings to their companions and devotees on the application. Clients can tweak their pictures with emoticon symbols, content, and drawing instruments. Some influencers on Snapchat boost their gathering of people individuals to draw in with them by just discharging Snaps temporarily.

Snaps are likewise transient – when a client sees a Snap picture or video, they just have a couple of moments with it before it's gone until the end of time. Clients can take screen captures of Snaps, yet the window for doing as such is constrained.

Contingent upon the kind of business you run, this could be a ground-breaking type of commitment for your gathering of people. In any case, Snapchat clients drift on the more youthful side, so except if you can catch the enthusiasm of this statistic, it may not be worth your time. Advertisers confront colossal strain to drive their brands' internet-based life commitment with their groups of onlookers, and it's fundamental not to sit around idly where your endeavors prove unproductive.

Gauge the Return on Investment

Each showcasing attempt ought to take a stab at a positive rate of return (ROI). Put just, in case you're not procuring more than what you put resources into a crusade methodology, that system isn't practical and most likely won't stay suitable for long. Snapchat is costly for publicists on account of the potential for high commitment levels.

Most customary publicizing models for Snapchat utilize an expense for every impression show. Basically, you pay for each time clients see your substance. Lamentably for advertisers keen on Snapchat, the stage isn't well disposed for little or developing organizations.

The base spends for publicizing on Snapchat is a stunning $40,000.

Extraordinary promotion models that work on an expense for each swipe show are likewise costly. Except if you have the liquidity to contribute that much for a possibly indeterminate result, the base purchase is a solid obstruction.

You could tailor your Snapchat promoting utilizing a remarkable geofilter for the savviest results. As the name proposes, a geofilter focuses on your substance to an explicit area. This can be viable for neighborhood organizations who need to contact more individuals in their general vicinity. Snapchat will consider the span of the territory you need to target and the evaluated activity volume amid an offered period to decide the expense.

Pick Your Audience

Generally, Snapchat just fills in as an advertising stage for business- to-client associations. In the event that you work in a business-to- business task, you in all probability won't discover enough expert nearness on Snapchat to legitimize putting resources into a showcasing effort. Snapchat is an immediate line to the end client. If you need to develop leads straightforwardly from your buyer base, you may discover them on Snapchat.

Likewise, think about what sort of merchandise and enterprises your organization offers. Do your optimal client types incline toward the more youthful side? Over 70% of Snapchat clients are more youthful than 34, so on the off chance that you take into account a more established market, you most likely won't see positive outcomes. On the off chance that your clients are youthful and acknowledge interactive media content, consider approaches to send them profitable substance in photograph or video organize.

In the event that you can think about a few potential outcomes, it might be an ideal opportunity to begin Snapchatting. Over 90% of battles using Snapchat report deals increase after promoting on the stage.

How Does Snapchat Compare with Various Social Media Strategies?

A standout amongst other apparatuses for advertisers on Snapchat is the capacity to transfer connections for your crowd. These connections touch base to clients in a simple to-explore arrangement. Clients just swipe up to see the substance. Snapchat reports that its swipe-up rate accomplishes multiple times more positive outcomes than normal navigate rates on other promoting channels.

Utilizing Snapchat connections, you can send your group of onlookers educational articles, email select ins, video content, solicitations to introduce your image's applications, connections to your site and other web-based social networking profiles, and significantly more.

If clients are occupied with your image, they'll likely set aside the opportunity to swipe up through your connections and see what you bring to the table. On the off chance that you tailor your Snapchat battle to catching the consideration of a more youthful customer base, you could conceivably expand your image mindfulness.

Campaigning with Snapchat

Each business has an interesting identity, and your promoting endeavors on a fun-focused stage like Snapchat should feature your human side. Consider the accompanying when concocting better approaches to connect with your group of onlookers:

Talk one-on-one with clients. You may get messages, questions, or reactions about your advertising materials from clients. Consider this input important and try to react to whatever number of client commitment as could be expected under the circumstances. Current buyers love to feel esteemed, so indicate them you care by setting aside the opportunity to exclusively address their worries and react to their remarks.

Insider looks. Demonstrate your group of onlookers what goes ahead of the camera at your organization. In the event that you create merchandise, consider completing a stroll through your generation office to demonstrate to your clients how you make your items. You could likewise have cheerful substance demonstrating your representatives making the most of their time at work and featuring a portion of the things that makes your organization special.

Work with influencers. Online networking influencers have enormous reach, so search for Snapchat identities with sizeable followings who create content identified with your image. When you find a couple of competitors, approach them with cross-limited time thoughts and check whether you can profit by access to their substantial groups of onlookers.

Keep in contact. More youthful individuals are commonly present on world occasions. Data ventures rapidly, and youngsters regard organizations that can deliver something profitable that resounds

with the occasions. Try not to race to post content about the most recent patterns and occasions, be that as it may. Numerous organizations have experienced grievous kickback their clients over heartless or ineffectively coordinated substance discharges via web- based networking media, so utilize prudence when choosing what to transfer.

Don't Get Lazy

Another imperative certainty to hold up under as a main priority (at any rate until further notice) is that numerous advertisers still can't seem to understand the potential Snapchat has as a showcasing resource. Your rivals might not have considered promoting on Snapchat because of the staggering impact Facebook and Twitter have had throughout the years. Numerous experts have expelled it as a straightforward photograph sharing application for young people.

Snapchat is definitely in excess of a period of executioner for young people. Innumerable brands have had achievement advertising on the stage. If you can tailor a publicizing model to your financial plan and objectives, you simply need to create Snapchat-accommodating substance to begin receiving the benefits.

Pinterest

Pinterest can be one of the more overlooked social media platforms. For the most part, Pinterest ranks lower than the top social media companies when it comes to monthly active users. This can often lead it to be seen as growing increasingly irrelevant, especially by those who are just starting out in the social media marketing world. However, while it is true that Pinterest is a smaller platform, Pinterest has an advantage that the other social media platforms don't. Pinterest users primarily use the platform to plan out what they want to purchase in advance.

This has tremendous implications. The first and foremost is that consumers don't actively avoid sales pitches or images meant to promote products.

Since Pinterest is primarily a consumer platform, you will have greater levels of opportunity to share and sell your products. People who visit Pinterest are open-minded, often looking to the site for opportunities to embark on new projects, look for new products and otherwise improve their own lives. They are searching for recipes, ideas, decorations and projects that will occupy their time.

When Pinterest users find a post that they like, they will pin it to their collection, known as their board. Boards are often separated by users into different types, depending on the overall purpose the user has for that board. For example, decoration pins could be pinned the board labeled "New House." This board may also include housing designs, furniture and other types of posts that would be thematically appropriate to set up a new house. Once they have pinned a post, they will be able to revisit it whenever they like. Furthermore, people can see each other's board and draw inspiration from them.

This creates a highly concentrated network of individuals who are most likely to make purchasing decisions. While they might not necessarily convert immediately, the act of adding a pin to the board will serve as a reminder that specific products or ideas exist. This can be extremely valuable for your brand, especially if one of your products is pinned to a board. That essentially serves as a reminder to potential customers that your product exists. This increases the chances of conversion.

Pinterest is an exceptional platform when it comes to business to consumer relations. You can promote your own brands, create interesting and engaging pins and even create your own boards for consumers to follow along. Let's take a look at each of the features that Pinterest offers to business owners.

Pins:

In Pinterest, a post is referred to as a pin. A pin is either a photo or a video that you upload. Unlike other social media sites, when you click on the pin itself, you will be taken to a link of the original picture's website. So, this is a great way to help direct people to

your website organically. If a user sees a pin and wants to know more about it, they'll have the link take them to the direct source.

As a business user, you're going to be primarily relying on creating your own original pins in order to distribute over Pinterest. Pins have descriptors that you can write. When writing in these descriptions, it's important to include accurate and relevant keywords, writing them out as hashtags so that others can find your content.

Boards:

Pins go on boards. A board is a thematic collection of pins, created by users. You'll most likely want to create your own boards, varying them based on different themes and ideas that are relevant to your business. Remember, other Pinterest users will be able to find your boards, so make sure that they are relevant to your target demographics interests.

Advertising:

One of the bigger challenges in Pinterest is discovery. There are a lot of pins constantly being put up and it can be easy for your pins to get lost in the shuffle. Organic searches only go so far. If you want to ensure that your pins are actually seen by users, you're going to want to take advantage of Pinterest's advertising engine.

The primary method of using Pinterest for advertising is creating what's known as Promoted Pins. A promoted pin is just the same as a regular pin, except that it will be displayed in front of relevant users. Just like any other advertising engine, the target can be highly specific, and you will be able to increase your reach than if you were just to use organic marketing.

In order to create promoted pins or videos, you'll need to create a Pinterest for Business account, or just simply switch over your regular Pinterest account to a business account. This is free and can be done quickly.

Once you have a Pinterest for Business account, you'll not only be able to create campaigns to run promoted pins, you'll also be able to evaluate the metrics that Pinterest provides. Pinterest keeps track of

how many people click on your pins, which pins get the most views and other such important metrics. You'll need these when it comes to evaluating the efficiency of the pins you are posting.

Who Is Pinterest Best for?

Pinterest is best for businesses that are looking to increase their brand authority, sell products to consumers and generate awareness. The majority of Pinterest users are women, who are also the primary decision-makers when it comes to consumer decisions for a household. A significantly smaller userbase of men exist and use Pinterest on a daily or monthly basis.

So, if you are looking to sell products that skew towards women or is geared directly at women, Pinterest is one of the best possible platforms you can use.

Pinterest Categories

While Pinterest has a wide array of categories and users can create pins about whatever topic they like, some categories are considered to be the primary drivers behind Pinterest. If you have a business that is relevant or adjacent to these categories, you will have a significantly easier time entering the Pinterest market. However, if you find that your products fall outside of these categories, you might not see them as promising results. This doesn't necessarily mean you won't be able to find success in using Pinterest, it's just that you won't know the degrees of success until you try it out. Let's look at the top 8 categories in Pinterest for 2019.

Travel:

Travel is the unabashed king of Pinterest in 2019. Pinterest enables those with a wanderlust to find great deals, learn about different and interesting places in the world and live vicariously through other travelers. In fact, according to Pinterest, a traveler is more likely to use Pinterest to make travel plans and decisions than a typical travel agency.

Health and Wellness:

Fitness, living a healthy lifestyle and food recipes are extremely popular on Pinterest. 2019 continues the modern trend of individuals continually seeking to live healthier and more productive lives. With health and wellness being such a large category, those who have health products to sell or fitness routines to share on their blogs are getting quite a bit of attention.

Hobbies and Interests:

Pinterest users who are interested in hobbies are primarily focused on arts and crafts. Things such as painting, pottery and gardening are extremely popular categories in 2019. People often look to Pinterest in the hopes of getting inspiration for the next hobby to pursue and as such, there are plenty of opportunities to advertise in specific hobby niches.

Celebrations:

Weddings and birthdays have a large number of elements to them, from decorations to ideas, to cakes. Pinterest users often look for inspiration and instructions on how to make the most out of their special occasions, using Pinterest sources to find recipes for these celebrations.

Food:

While health and wellness may contain a large number of recipes, food as a standalone category comes in 5th place for most popular. People are always on the hunt for all sorts of recipes to use, ranging from a hybrid paleo-vegan diet known as Pegan, to simple bread baking tips.

Home Projects:

Another extremely popular category for Pinterest is Do It Yourself projects, mostly pertaining to home and garden. People are looking for either inspiration to create new looks for their homes or are searching for practical, step by step advice on how to create specific types of furniture.

Men's Style:

While men might not make up a large percentage of Pinterest, they do, however, still make purchasing decisions, especially when it comes to personal style. Men's style comes in at the 7th most popular category for 2019, which indicates a trend of more and more men coming to look at style as something to be concerned with.

Women's Style:

Coming after men's style, women are still using Pinterest to look for new clothes and style ideas. One area that is trending in this category is sustainable fashion, as more and more consumers are becoming conscious of the toll that certain types of fashion products can have on the environment.

CHAPTER 6 IGNITE PASSION AND TRANSCEND FEAR

Starting a new YouTube channel is not an easy task; however, follow these tips on starting a channel and you will surely gain a devoted audience!

Describe "Success" as a YouTuber

Before uploading your first work, make sure you truly understand the reason for behind the YouTube channel and why you created it:

Providing value for your audience while earning a profit from them

Whatever the reason may be for starting this YouTube channel, you should recognize your outlook and how you define "success". This would provide you with a goal to aim towards. This will also push and persuade you to attain that goal. Having a goal that was tough to achieve would only serve to demotivate you. Set your goals as small achievable targets and you will be able to reevaluate your position when these goals are met. If you set your initial goal as "I want to make $1 million", very few broadcasters will achieve this. However,

if you set your first goal as "I want 100 viewers on one of my broadcasts", this is much more achievable and will serve as motivation to achieve this goal.

Recognize Your Viewers

Knowing your audience is the key to the success of your YouTube channel. This means you need to familiarize yourself with the audience who would be interested in viewing the videos you upload. It is crucial to understand the interests and hobbies of your target audience.

Once you are familiarized with your audience, you could then produce the videos relevant to their needs. Remember, the significance of your video is directly proportional to the viewership and subscription of your channel. You can glean a lot of information about your viewers from the comments they leave on your YouTube videos but this doesn't really give a full profile of your viewers. Thankfully, YouTube provides you with the tools to analyze this information.

Being Passionate About the Content You Are Creating

Starting a YouTube channel just because you assume that it would benefit you financially is meaningless. There are a lot of different platforms that can help you earn money, however, if you don't have the zeal for it, your viewers would just have a glimpse of it and straight away identify that you're not passionate about it.

Not just that, if you are not really passionate about this task that you're doing, you would not have any internal drive to do it day in and day out. You need to believe in the content you are delivering. If you give the persona that you aren't really that interested, this is going to put the viewer in the same mindset and reduce the chances of them returning to your channel in the future.

Being Knowledgeable on the Content You Are Creating

Being passionate about a subject is one thing but if you don't have an in-depth knowledge of what you are presenting, your content is going to be very shallow and will not hold the attention of your

audience. You need to convince the audience that you are a specialist on your subject and that they are going to learn something that they didn't know before they viewed your broadcast.

The Attitude Should Be Positive

Audience and subscribers need a story that has a "feel good" factor, therefore just concentrate on the positivity. Keep away from complaints and constant rages. Rather, "look on the brighter side."

That is not to say that you can't highlight any issues or faults with what you are presenting but you must stay calm at all times and refrain from saying anything that could be deemed as libelous or illegal.

Constant rages may get you a reputation that will attract some subscribers, just to see you "go off on one", however, this will hurt your brand and ultimately, your ability to earn.

Even though you know your subject, you must be careful so as not to come across as arrogant. Be humble and assume that the viewer has some intelligence and understanding of what you are telling them. There is nothing worse as a viewer than being made to feel inadequate by a condescending presenter.

Be Confident in Your Presenting Skills

So, you are passionate about your subject and you have enough knowledge to be called a specialist in your field, but these qualities will be lost if you haven't got the presentation skills to convey your knowledge to your viewers.

Getting your voice to a tone and volume that you are happy with could take a lot of time if you are not used to giving presentations or public speaking. This is one skill that you will need to hone before you can even consider publishing your first video. The way your voice comes across will say a lot about you and your channel so speak clearly, speak slowly and speak confidently.

Your Channel Should Be Different

To make a unique channel amongst the numerous people who are willing to start a channel, you need to be different, unique and novel. Think of vast ideas and thoughts and stick to them. This would also help you differentiate your channel.

If you can find a niche area of the market and your broadcasts are of sufficient quality, you really could get a massive viewer base. This is a fine line however. If you go for something too unique, there are not going to be enough viewers who are interested in your content so do your research before deciding on a final subject area. Make use of the YouTube search facility to see how many other channels are out there similar to the one that you are proposing to create. If you do manage to find any, make a note of how many views they receive and then determine as to whether you think you could make a better job of securing viewers.

Connecting with Other Creators

The most essential tip for a YouTube creator is to connect, network and make connections with other YouTube creators in their niches. By connecting with other creators who share similar interests, you are more likely to pick up some of their viewers which will be vital in the early days of your channel's life. You are starting from scratch so you need to get viewers into your channel through any means possible. What better way than to target people who you already know have some interest in the material you will be broadcasting?

Make positive comments on the videos of creators of similar subjects to your own. Give these comments some substance rather than just saying "nice video". This will get you known to viewers who may then click on your profile and watch some of your videos. Hopefully, they will like them enough to hit that subscribe button.

In fact, the YouTube broadcaster will need to reinvent themselves several times to ensure that their approach stays fresh and that viewers are not subjected to the same format for each broadcast. Once you've done the hard work in engaging a viewer, you need to go the extra mile in order to keep them.

CHAPTER 7 BEGINNERS MISTAKES AND WHAT TO DO INSTEAD

There are common mistakes that most affiliate marketers make when they first get started. Fortunately, most of these mistakes can be corrected so that many affiliates will go on to become very successful.

What is most successful is to learn to avoid these mistakes from the beginning.

The most common mistakes beginners make include the following: Not doing SEO and social media marketing

Many online marketers think that building a website will naturally bring tons of traffic to check it out. The truth is that you need time to build a website's online reputation. It also takes time before your website gets decent search engine results on target keywords.

To get an optimal amount of website traffic, you need to optimize your content for the search engines and share each post to your social networks.

Spreading their energy on too many websites

Some affiliates try to maximize the bandwidth limit of their hosting service by making many websites. These websites act more like nets designed to capture people and direct them to one main website and most people don't like that.

For your websites to attract the right people, you need to make sure that the content you post is useful to your target audience. It is best to take your time and develop one great website that attracts a loyal base of customers than have a lot of websites that put people off from buying what you promote.

Choosing bad products to market

It is easier to sell products that have a great reputation because they are basically selling themselves. You don't need much persuasion to sell reputable products and you will make your customers happy so they are willing to buy more from you in the future. If you sell a poor product though, you will get a bad reputation and lose business.

Linking directly to the landing page of advertisers

Other affiliate marketers just post their affiliate links around the internet hoping that they will get a good catch. This is not a good strategy because people seldom buy from links they find in a forum or a comment.

Instead, you will find great success if you follow the selling process to be able to make a sale consistently. What this means is that instead of posting affiliate links around the internet, you need to focus your marketing efforts on leading people back to your website where you can build a relationship with them.

What to do instead - 3 RIGHT ways to get started

Now that you know what the most common mistakes are, let's look at what you should be doing instead of making those errors.

Select the right niche

If you want to build an online marketing career, you need to choose a topic that you are good at or feel passionate about. Having an interest in the subject that you are discussing on your website, blog and newsletters will get other people excited and you need their excitement in order to make sales.

If you are not interested in what you are writing, you will become frustrated, bored and may even give up. If you love what you are selling though, your work will be happy for you and you will stay motivated.

Solve your prospect buyers' problems

Potential buyers have problems that they want to solve and your entire job is to solve those problems through the products and services you are marketing as an affiliate. All you need to do is to help them realize that the product that you are promoting is the best solution to their problems.

Learn about the product you are selling

You can't sell a product consistently if you don't know what sets them apart from similar products in the same niche. The best way to learn about a product is by using it. If there is no way for you to buy the product, you should at least research what other people are saying about it.

10 tips for ALL successful affiliate marketers

Now that you know a few ways to help optimize your efforts in becoming a successful affiliate marketer, let's look at 10 additional ways:

Make use of all types of free advertising

There are free ways to advertise your online presence in a way that will build the engagement you need to promote effectively. For instance, you could create a Facebook page and develop a following by engaging with relevant, but non-competitive businesses. You could also make use of forums and free bookmarking websites like Reddit and Pinterest. Online listing websites like Craigslist are also useful.

Don't be afraid to use paid advertising

If your website is already earning, you could use part of the profits for paid online advertising. There are a variety of advertising opportunities that are affordable and highly effective, such as social media advertising. You should only use this option though if you are certain that it will increase the sales of your website.

Focus on creating relationships and building trust rather than making sales

In all your marketing strategies, you should focus on building your authority and forging long-lasting relationships. People who trust you will consider your suggestion to buy when you present them with your affiliate link.

Learn the different aspects of affiliate marketing one at a time

As a beginner, try to avoid getting overwhelmed by all the information. Instead, focus on your goal, which is to build your online reputation and to make a sale. For example, you could forget about email marketing in the beginning and focus on creating valuable blog content.

By the time you are done learning about creating valuable content, you will already have a decent list to start learning about email marketing. Not only will that keep you from feeling overwhelmed, but your efforts will be smarter because you will have taken more time to learn one thing at a time.

Improve your email list

Think of your email list as a regular reader of your posts, engage them with thoughtful information, polls and other opportunities to feel heard and appreciated by you. This way, they will be more likely to read your posts and look forward to receiving your emails.

Assess your strategy regularly

Your strategy should evolve as you learn new things about affiliate marketing. This means constantly looking for better strategies that will improve your conversion rate. There are many sources for learning affiliate marketing online.

Create feedback of the products you are selling

An effective way to sell your products is by writing feedback. You could also create a video feedback about it and post it on YouTube to reach more people. Make sure that your videos have links that will lead visitors back to your blog.

Create a daily marketing routine

The number of tasks that you need to accomplish every day may overwhelm you if you do not organize them. Try to create a daily and weekly schedule on what you should accomplish. This is the best way for you to keep up with your affiliate marketing tasks.

Keep learning

You should keep learning if you want to be a competitive affiliate marketer in your niche. Remember that the online world is always changing. To keep up with the changes and stay ahead of the competition, it will be in your best interest to constantly look for information that will help you improve your sales.

You will find it helpful to look into the trends of online marketing and your niche. To do this, you will learn a lot from the gurus of online marketing. Pay attention to who they are and follow them on social networking websites.

Be patient

Lastly, you should be patient with this industry. It takes time to learn and to create effective systems that convert visitors to buyers. There is no need to get frustrated when you are not getting your expected results, it just means to keep working at it and continually improve your strategies.

The more experience you get, the more money you will make. Also, as you build your business sales will grow all the time if you pay attention and follow the suggestions you've been learning about so far.

CONCLUSION

Be aware that to run a great shopping website once you successfully take the plunge into creating a website for the company there is going to need to be security for every single piece of information that comes through the seller's website. Take care of these things with certificates that will encrypt your URL and links so that breaches will not try and attack the assets of your company and possibly even crash the whole site is complete and take everything.

Utilize marketing tools like Google AdWords and Facebook ads to gain full exposure to the community that you are engaging with. Remember that the community is going to be an online base so there needs to be consistency if the members begin to become forgetful. Entice them with special offers and make every customer feel great when they come to your shop so that they know they are getting more out of it than any other shop they will trust.

Now that you have made it to the end of this book, you hopefully have an understanding of how to get started creating your own passive income stream with FBA, as well as a strategy or two, or three, that you are anxious to try for the first time. Before you go ahead and start giving it your all, however, it is important that you have realistic expectations as to the level of success you should expect in the near future.

While it is perfectly true that some people experience serious success right out of the gate, it is an unfortunate fact of life that they are the exception rather than the rule. What this means is that you should expect to experience something of a learning curve, especially when you are first figuring out what works for you. This is perfectly normal, however, and if you persevere you will come out the other side better because of it.

The next step is to stop reading and to start doing whatever is required of you to ensure that yourself and those you care about will be on good financial grounds and stability. If you find that you still need help getting started you will likely have better results by creating a schedule that you hope to follow including personal milestones and practical applications for various parts of the tasks as well as the overall process of acquiring the life-changing knowledge and experiences.

In this light, studies show that complex tasks that are broken down into individual pieces, including individual targets, have a much greater chance of being completed when compared to something that has a general need of being completed but no real time table for doing so. Even though it would seem silly, go ahead and set your own deadlines for completion, complete with indicators of success and failure. After you have successfully completed all of your required milestones, you will be glad you took that former step

Once you have finished the initial process it is important to understand that it is just that, only part of a larger plan of preparation. Your best chances for overall success will come by taking the time to learn as many vital skills as possible. Only by using your prepared status as a springboard to greater profit margins will you be able to truly rest soundly knowing that you are finally taking the right steps into realizing your financial balance and stability, not to mention prosperity.

You need to practice. You need experience deciphering market patterns and you need to be constantly tweaking your if-then statements for your trading setups. Every day is a new game and a new puzzle to solve. As I've mentioned, many people believe that trading can be reduced to a few rules that they can follow every morning. Always do this or always do that. You must learn how to think in day trading, and this is no easy task.

You must start recognizing patterns and developing trading strategies. And these strategies must be practiced in real time and under stress. Trading in simulators can help and is absolutely necessary, but there is no substitute for trading with your real hard–earned cash where your results actually matter.

When you begin as a trader, you most likely will be horrible. Many times, at the beginning of my career I came to the conclusion that day trading was not for me. Even now that I am an experienced and profitable trader, there is at least one day almost every month that I wonder if I can trade in this market any longer. Of course, this feeling of disappointment goes away faster these days, usually after the next good trade. But for you, because you have not seen success yet, surviving the learning curve is very difficult. I know that. However, this does not mean you should lose a lot of money when you trade live at the beginning. Trading in the simulators will help to prepare you for real trading with real money.

Lightning Source UK Ltd.
Milton Keynes UK
UKHW020215080521
383350UK00003B/265